'UN-CONVENTIONAL'

MONEY SECRETS

"We help guarantee your retirement, we help guarantee your future."TM

By Gregory Pavlidis

I wish to thank my family and my dearest friends for putting up
with my long hours during the writing of this book. ☺

Contents

Introduction

Basically, everything you read here today, has one theme in common, how to protect yourself and become 'Financially Fit'.

Like any fitness routine that has a prayer of working **for you, you must** become **involved.** You **must** learn the very things that **we** know and implement them as something that comes from **your own** newly gained knowledge. The trainer who has a client who just 'shows up' once a week, or a few times a week, but does **not** take **ownership** of the new lifestyle of health and fitness, and instead, binges, and lies around on the couch the rest of the time, will **never** succeed, even with the best of trainers. **You** need to change your financial lifestyle, and the **first** step is **to learn** what **we are teaching you.**

Our mission is to share financial information that is 'off the radar' and 'unconventional', even 'controversial' and by doing so, we will continue to save people and their families one person at a time. We are sharing information that is so buried, or off the radar, that it is **really** hard to find. And most of the things that break through the surface are completely inaccurate, defaming and slanderous. But, that's not our battle. We don't fight, we educate, and hope that when presented with proven facts, our students, who learn our *Un-conventional Money Secrets*, will be able to understand the difference between unsubstantiated propaganda, and fact based educational material. Furthermore, our specialty is researching these *hidden financial facts*, and through the courageousness of educational companies like ProfessorIT.com for allowing us to bring this information *into the light*, you now have a fighting chance for a bright future!

There are a few good people out there who *do* tell the truth, people like Dr. David Babbel, Ed Slott, Tony Robbins, R. Nelson Nash, Barry Kaye, Robert Kiyosaki, Brett Kitchen & Ethan Kap, MJ DeMarco, Harry Dent Jr., and of course, John Bogle & me.

The information that we bring to light, is not exactly a *secret*, but the Main Stream so called 'financial professionals' and 'gurus' out there would rather that you **not know** the information we are telling you. Why? Because they make **zillions** of dollars off of you by keeping your money 'in the market' and under **their** management. Remember, **they** make money whether you win **or** lose, and behind closed doors they are **laughing** at everyone and how much money they are making off of **your losses!** There is a book called "F.I.A.S.C.O: Blood In The Water On Wall Street", by Frank Partnoy, which talks about just that subject! It is written by a former derivatives trader, a former 'insider', and it is a well written, accurate yet disgusting tale of thievery.

To his credit he **really** blows the whistle!

There is **no need** to be a **victim anymore!** Take control of your financial life! **Guarantee your retirement!** Shield your money from **taxes!** Most of all women and women's groups should empower themselves with information from this book & books like it. After the baby boomers, you (women) are the next largest most successful demographic, and statistics show you want to learn more about finances but as it stands, you know very little. We love & support women as a group! So by **all means**, pick up the phone and **call us** for your **free** consultation!

Our number is: 877-855-1881

gregory@BeverlyHillsPrivatePensions.com

We are here to teach you, and to help you.

Have a great day! ☺

Further books to read if you REALLY wish to DIVE IN!

1. *13 Bankers: the Wall Street Takeover and the NEXT Financial Meltdown by Simon Johnson and James Kwak.*
2. *Myths, Lies, and Downright Stupidity by John Stossel*
3. *The Creature from Jeckyll Island by G. Edward Griffin "It's not Federal. There is no reserve. And it is not a bank!"*
4. *The Pirates of Manhattan by Barry Dyke*
5. *The Trouble with Mutual Funds by Richard Rutner*
6. *Empire of Debt: The Rise of an Epic Financial Crisis by William Bonner and Addison Wiggin*
7. *Financial Reckoning Day – Surviving the Soft Depression of the 21st Century by William Bonner*

There are SO many more! Call us and we will give you the full list!

Now, before we get started, we just want to say, that although we personally have very strong opinions for one way of saving money for retirement, and very strong opinions against another way of 'saving', called "investing", it does not mean that we have anything against the reputable, hardworking people, who sell wall street investments. They just do not know any better. Who knows, maybe this educational book will enlighten and prompt some "Wall Streeter's" to jump on over to the safe side of the street! We honestly believe that everyone...

E-v-e-r-y-o-n-e... does the best that s/he can do, based on the knowledge, experience and unique brain chemistry and consciousness that one possesses at any particular moment in time. And although that action may not be 'right' for themselves, or for anyone else, whatever that action may be... we believe if people knew better, people would do better.

Haven't you ever had a time in your life when you were absolutely certain about something – so certain you would have bet anything on it? And then, sometime later, some new piece of information presented itself to you, and/or you all of a sudden saw it in a new light, and whammo! What you were once certain, 'was', you are now certain was great or the best, was really, really far from it. Thank god for new evidence, and changing perspectives! The saddest is when people get caught up in the same illness of destructive behaviors over and over again and....

expect different results - that is what Einstein calls insanity, and I agree with him! That's really an addiction, isn't it? When a person repeats the same destructive behavior or behaviors, over again, and expects different results... That illness can be with finances, with relationships, and drugs. It's a very sad condition, especially for those who think they're above it, and have it all worked out, nice and neatly. But there are many fine groups out there to help those who need any variety of behavioral modifications, just ask!

Anyway, our objective is only to present factual, provable and accurate information that will hopefully enlighten many people to some often used, but little publicized ways to save money and protect retirements. So please read with pleasure and openness and with a light heart, whether or not you are absolutely certain we are right, or absolutely certain we are wrong.

Live Long and Prosper. ☺

CHAPTER I

The Philosophy
Of Investing

At its core the basic premise or philosophy of investing is really very simple.

4-Step Formula:

1. Save Money
2. Earn Compound Interest (i.e. *Save Money at an Accelerated Rate*),
3. Never lose MONEY, and
4. Avoid taxes, legally.

If you can do these four things your retirement dollars will grow rapidly and beyond your expectations!

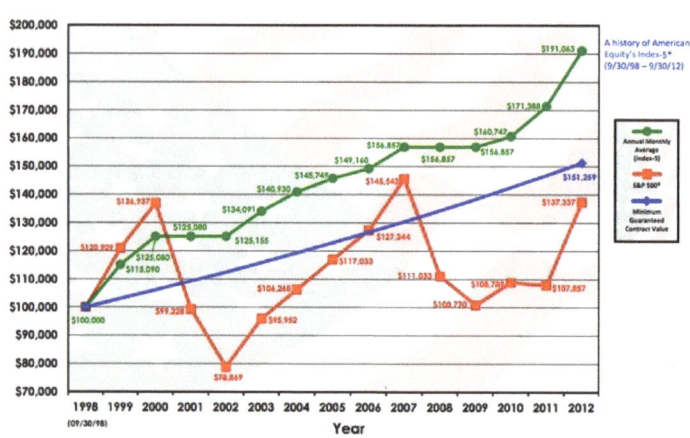

Should You Go For The Highest Returns Possible? The Highest Risk? Here's Why That Is Simply Not Necessary, And Down-Right Not Even Advisable!

Most of the time we are lured, or duped, into believing that we have to shoot for the highest returns possible in the stock market. This is simply not true. We do not have to buy into high risk in order to NET a high gain.

I will prove this mathematically.

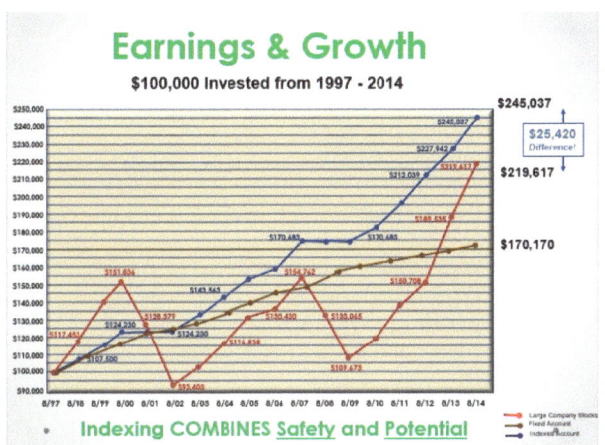

First, to clarify some key points:

1. & 2. Save Money And Earn Compound Interest

One must take advantage of **compound interest** in order to save at an accelerated rate. (Albert Einstein called compound interest The 8th Wonder of The World, And **The Most Powerful Force In The Universe**).

Why? Due especially to **inflation** (the invisible tax) and the **ever rising regular income taxes**, it is necessary to use compound interest to keep pace with, or preferably, **outpace the other two.**

Compound Interest-The Rule of 72

Simply divide the number 72 by your expected rate of return to determine the number of years it will take your money to double.

Age	4%	Age	6%	Age	8%	Age	12%
Money doubles every 18 years		Money doubles every 12 years		Money doubles every 9 years		Money doubles every 6 years	
29	$10,000	29	$10,000	29	$10,000	29	$10,000
47	$20,000	41	$20,000	38	$20,000	35	$20,000
65	$40,000	53	$40,000	47	$40,000	41	$40,000
		65	$80,000	56	$80,000	47	$80,000
				65	$160,000	53	$160,000
						59	$320,000
						65	$640,000

"The most powerful force in the universe is compound interest." [1]

"The person that understands compound interest will earn it. The person that does not will pay it!" [2]

- Albert Einstein

3. Never Lose

In the Fixed Indexed Annuity (FIA), Maximum Tax-Advantaged Life Insurance (MTA) and 412(e)(3) videos that I made, you WILL see how **it is possible to keep every dime**, and to earn more than enough for retirement lifetime!

Warren Buffet has two main rules for success:

1. Never Lose Money.

2. Never Forget Rule # 1.

5. **Avoid Income Taxes Legally**

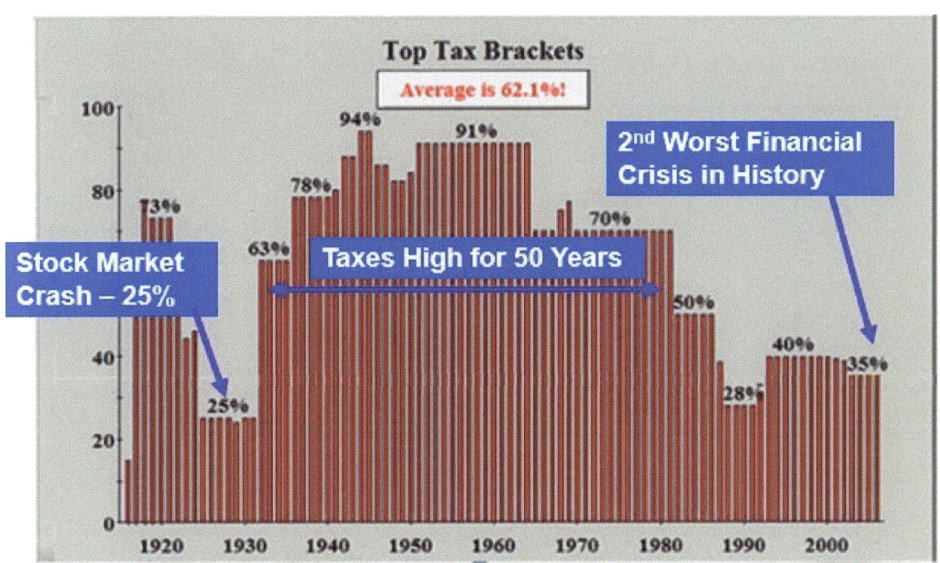

And of course, (sometimes) **avoiding income taxes on distribution** (not evading them), **increases your net income quite significantly**. Example: If your tax rate is 33%, then you need to **earn** 50% more just to offset that income tax! So, if you do not have to pay income tax, it is like an automatic gain of 50% or more! Now **that** is a **great** Return On Investment (ROI).

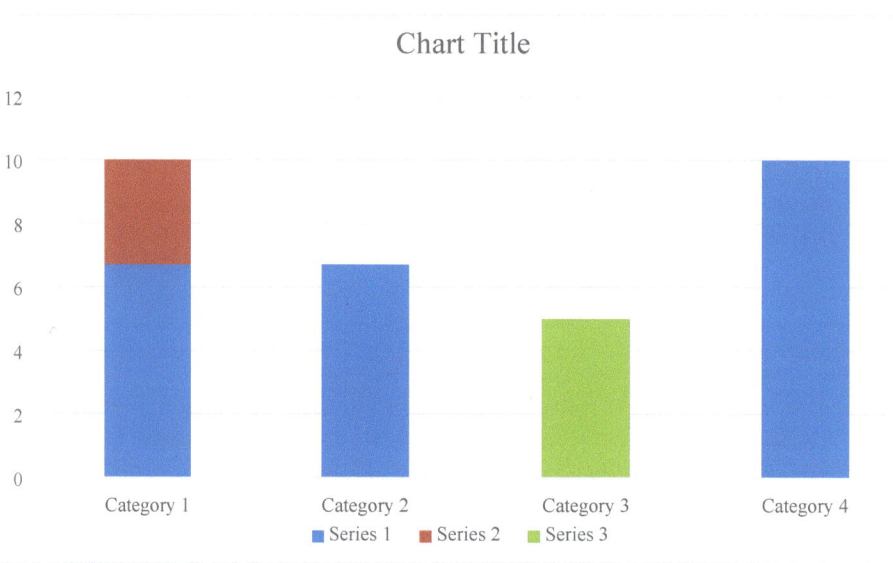

In the Chart above, you can see that in C1, if your income is 10 (blue), your tax is about 33% (red). In C2, you can see what you are left with after taxes (blue). In C3, you can see the green which represents the approx. 50%, you would need to earn back, in order to just break even, after getting hit with 33% in taxes! And, in C4, you can see what your money would look like, if you did not have to pay tax on distribution.

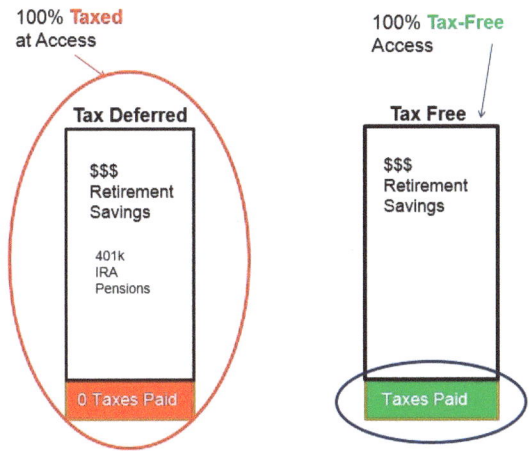

Tax Strategies

100% Taxed at Access

100% Tax-Free Access

Tax Deferred

$$$ Retirement Savings

401k IRA Pensions

0 Taxes Paid

Tax Free

$$$ Retirement Savings

Taxes Paid

How Do I Avoid Losses? Some Examples:

Let's take 7 five year periods and use $100,000 as an example.

Annualized Five-Year Returns

Period: S&P return FIA avg. return Number of FIA's Return Range

Period	S&P Return	FIA ave. return	No. of FIAs	Return Range
1997-2002	9.39%	9.19%	5	7.80% to 12.16%
1998-2003	-0.42%	5.46%	13	3.00% to 7.97%
1999-2004	-2.77%	4.69%	8	3.00% to 6.63%
2000-2005	-3.08%	4.33%	28	0.85% to 8.66%
2001-2006	5.11%	4.36%	13	1.91% to 6.55%
2002-2007	13.37%	6.12%	23	3.00% to 8.39%

| 2003-2008 | 3.18% | 6.05% | 19 | 3.00% to 7.80% |
| 2004-2009 | -1.05% | 4.19% | 27 | 2.25% to 6.83% |

(Chart from the Wharton Financial Institutions Center Personal Finance "Real World Indexed Annuity Returns" by Jack Marion, Geoffrey VanderPal, and [led by] Prof. David F. Babbel.)

If we do the calculations for the S&P 500 while being IN the stock market vs. NOT being in the market with a Roth IRA (FIA), MTA or 412(e)(3), our $100,000 grows to $126,212. Not bad, but oh! Uh, we forgot, assuming a 33% tax bracket and assuming a lump sum distribution, your $126,212 becomes $84,562!

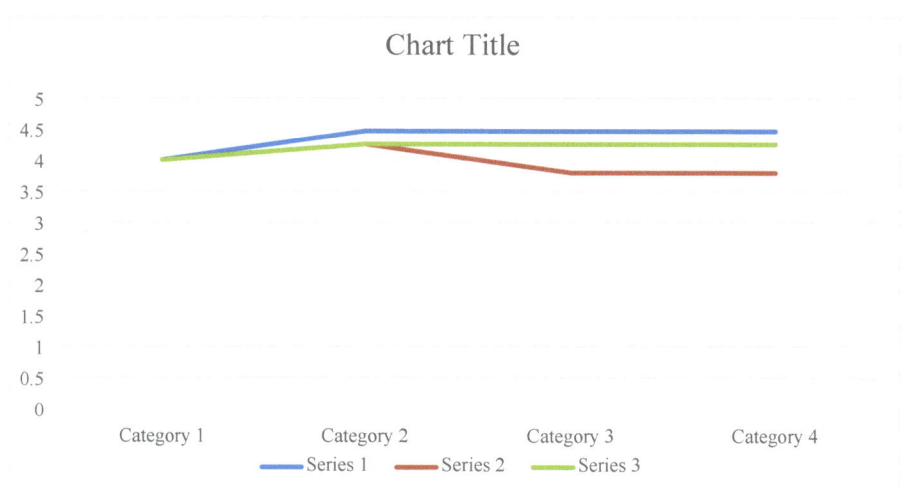

Blue = FIA (Safe, safe from Market Loss, and Taxes)
Green = Risky Money in The Market (S&P 500)
Red = Clobbered by Taxes and $ being in the market

In the graph above, you can see the blue line (FIA), beats the green line (S&P 500), and if the FIA is a ROTH too, it greatly exceeds the resulting gains the option of being in the market and getting taxed (red line) later!

In other words, if you had funded the same amount over time into a Roth IRA using an FIA you would have $147,715 and that is TAX FREE. **The difference** between your net of $84,562 (in the market) and your tax free Roth IRA (FIA, not in the market) of $147,715 **is 75%!**

Now, how does a 75% gain with no risk to principle AND/OR interest sound? Like Madoff? Hehe, no, it's JUST simple math.

You followed the simple math right here, yourself!
AND you did it mostly done by *avoiding* future taxes, and A**VOIDING** losses, and then by getting a modest return with a guaranteed cash accumulation vehicle.

So, summing it up, **save money, earn compound interest, never lose money, and avoid taxes, legally.** Easy, isn't it?!?!? ☺

CHAPTER II

Why do most people not know about this? What is the big secret?

Well, here it is. Again, we are not attorneys, do not know the thousands of pages of legal briefs, and to tell you the truth even if we did, who else does? [In July 2009, in the US Court of Appeals for the District of Columbia Circuit: a case was heard and remanded for reconsideration consistent with the Court's Opinion. In American Equity Investment Life Insurance Company et al v. SEC the Court granted the Petitions because the SEC's reasoning in its arguments was arbitrary and capricious, and thus illegal. The SECs Rule 151A stated that FIAs are not annuity contracts within the meaning of the Act and thus are subject to the SECs regulations. The SEC did not properly consider how this new categorization of the FIAs would affect efficiency, competition and capital formation.] This would have ultimately set up the SEC to regulate FIAs instead of the **better**, stronger, more efficient individual **state regulations that already exist**. So far, the SEC lost this battle to attempt to cull and isolate the FIAs from solely state run regulation which has done an admirable job since they were entrusted with the task, up to and including now.

We are going to break this down to its most basic components, as we always like to do.

There are two sides to the financial industry, the **variable** side which is regulated by the SEC (Securities Exchange Commission) and the **fixed** insurance side which is regulated by the individual states.

Variable means you can lose your money.   **Fixed** means your money is safe and **guaranteed**.

Unfortunately, the **variable** side is more mainstream, has more power, **more lobbyists,** and **much more advertising (which, by the way, is paid for by you, in the form of very high ongoing fees, most of which are hidden from you)**.   Has mainstream worked well for you?   No, obviously not, you have probably lost up to half your retirement savings! **[But you know about Mainstream/Wall Street – 'they' make sure you hear about it a lot through your employers, bankers, and television! Who pays the salaries for 'popular' TV personalities?   What commercials are aired during their shows?   Aren't these questions that should be asked?]**

Sometimes we get lucky, and the truth gets to briefly poke its head up into Mainstream Media, With Some Publications and news-people who have the guts to tell it the way it is…   Such as when, in a **2009 TIME magazine article by Stephen Gandel stated "The ugly truth, though, is that the 401(k) is a lousy idea, a financial flop, a rotten repository for our retirement reserves."**

Now, imagine *if you had known* about the fixed/SAFE side, and had your money in a Fixed **Indexed** Annuity (FIA) -- you would not have lost a DIME in any of the stock market catastrophes!

Can you imagine how good you'd feel???

TIME magazine's Stephen Gandel and former Harvard Professor Nancy Altman state: "…the best way to **GUARANTEE** a replacement for people's wages in retirement is by pooling risk, and the way to do that is through insurance."

Yet, now that the Madoffs of the world, have taken from our fair citizens **most** of their hard earned retirement money, the SEC (Securities Exchange Commission) had, back around 2006 to 2008, **engineered** a **move** and attempted to claim FIAs for their own regulation! **The very same SEC that was notified no less than (9) times to look into Madoff and each time the SEC was notified, the SEC dismissed any accusations against Madoff, and said he was a reputable broker!!! That was a $50 billion dollar catastrophe!**

Either they are THAT stupid, OR THAT corrupt! Either way, we wouldn't want them watching over our cup of loose change on the counter top! Would you?

On top of that, what was their premise with the lawsuit to control FIAs? Why did the SEC think it could take over this fantastic financial vehicle, the FIAs? The first was, they claimed that there was an **upside risk** in FIAs! Yup, you heard me correctly, they claimed there was an **upside risk**, and therefore it should be under SEC regulations. Can you imagine, claiming **"upside risk"** as a danger? Did you ever think about why on the SEC side of the fence, why they call a **giant crash** (loss of your money) in the Stock Market - **A CORRECTION! Really?!?!?** Yup, when people lose money, when you lose money in the Stock Market – they call it a

"Correction", as if gaining money is the wrong thing, and that losing money is the right thing! Holy smokes!

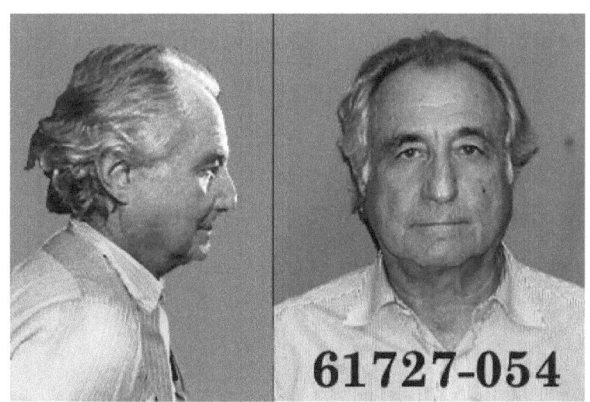

61727-054

And in any case, does it look like the SEC has really done **such an amazing** job with Madoff and all those like him…? Knowing what you know now, would you like to let such an agency take over the regulation of FIAs [**as well**]? Well, fortunately the courts do not believe it would be just for the SEC to take over the FIAs either.

On the flip side, how often have you heard of such **monumental scandals** in the fixed insurance industry? Sure, you get a few bad guys in any industry, but **never ever** to the **extent** that we have seen in the Madoff type of **scandal that** the SEC controlled and "regulated", **never**!

Are these the people [**--The "SEC"--**] the ones you want to oversee the regulation of your money? Or, would you rather have the **highly regulated**, **highly successful, states** oversee that your fixed, **guaranteed** money is safe?

By the way, **more verifiable facts: Insurance Companies are 100% Legal Reserve Companies. That means that, by law, every dollar they have promised to a client, they must have that same dollar in**

reserve to honor that promise. In contrast, Banks are only required to keep 10% in reserve for every dollar they loan out! If you tried to do that – you'd be arrested and hauled off to jail! Hehe, and because the stock market has no guarantees at all, there are no requirements for reserves! If you lose it, too bad, it's gone – you knew the risks! That's what they tell you, isn't it?

Let's get back to safety. Each state has a State Guarantee Association for the Insurance Companies. This fund is paid for by the legal reserve dollars that insurance companies are required to keep to do business in that state. And in the event of an insurance company failure (which there has only been a less than 1% failure rate in over 400 years! No other industry can even come close to that kind of success!), if other insurance companies don't purchase it for pennies on a dollar, and honor all the contracts (which they usually do), the State Guarantee Association keeps money for just such occasions. There are limits, so please see your individual State Guarantee Association for your State specific amounts.

Okay, we're a little passionate about this topic, please excuse us. But **injustices and cover-ups** just rub us the wrong way!

Hopefully, what we have presented to you, has given you reason to think, **and re-think** what you have been advised to do [**by the mainstream financiers**]. And hopefully, you now know that there are better ways to secure your future.

CHAPTER III

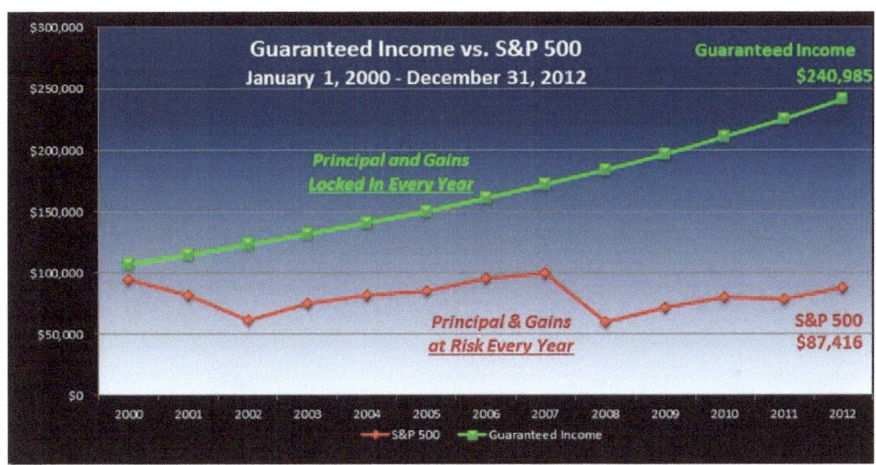

Two Separate And Unique Cash Accumulation Vehicles Offered By Life Insurance Companies

I. The Fixed Indexed Annuity -- Protection Of Gain With Guarantee Against Loss

If you like the idea of the upside potential of the stock market, but fear the downside risk, a vehicle which may be the answer for you is an **"FIA"** **(Fixed Indexed Annuity).**

What is this?

It is a type of annuity, and an **annuity** is a series of income payments made at regular intervals by an insurance company. A fixed annuity is as similarly safe as a "CD" (**Certificate of Deposit**), which is a savings vehicle with a bank.

A **Fixed Indexed Annuity** is a **Fixed Annuity** which links your gains to the upside potential of the stock market while eliminating the downside risk, because you are not *actually* ***in the market***.

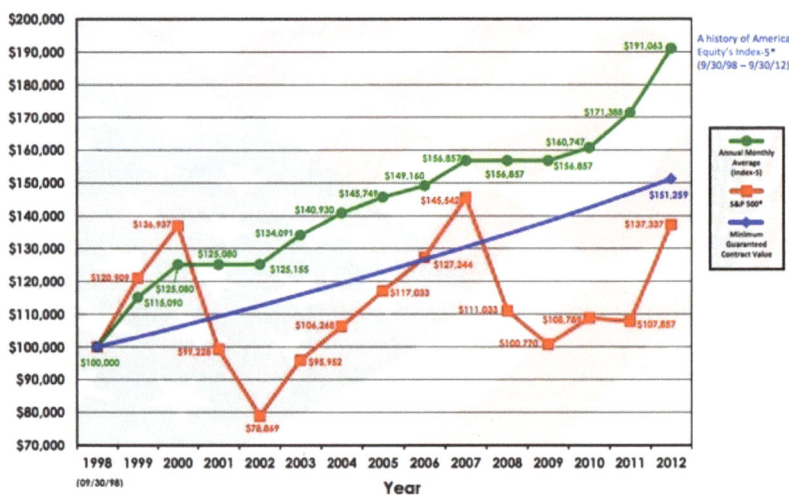

What Color Line Would You Prefer To Be On?

NOTE: Limiter:

This is not the time or place to help any of you to attempt a thorough understanding of the intricacies of the stock market and its management, fee structuring etc. We are going to assume you, the readership, have at least a basic knowledge of all of that (or that you will research it on your own) and my focus here is limited to explaining this very special vehicle.

Details Of The Fixed Indexed Annuity

Though they come in many different shapes and sizes, here, we will briefly cover some KEY facts that pertain to all of them.

1. *Your entire* **principal** *earns interest because there are* **no fees for the base contract**.
2. *When the market goes up, you share in the gain (and yes, there is a cap, meaning a limitation as to how high your share of a gain will be).*
3. *When the market goes down, you remain the same*

* (Like any long term financial vehicle, there is a surrender charge if cashed out before the end of the contract, **and there is never any market loss, because you are not in the market**). And regarding surrender charges - get over it. YES! You are charged if you break your word to the company, and I imagine you would demand financial compensation for anyone breaking a financial agreement with you - right?

EXAMPLE: IF you invested $100,000, and the stock market in general gained 10%, your total new principal plus interest would be $110,000. AND typically if the stock market lost 10% on the next cycle, your new total principal plus interest would be $99,000 i.e., you would have also lost 10%. Let's reflect for a moment on how devastating the actual losses were in 2008 for many people -- **losing up to 50% of their entire life savings** in a matter of days, weeks or months.

Not So With A Fixed Indexed Annuity!!!

No one with a Fixed Indexed Annuity lost a dime!! Not one dime!!!

How And Why?

The use of Stock Options makes this possible.

Stock options explained:

The insurance company sets aside only a small portion (let's say about 0.06 cents) of every dollar placed in the **FIA** to buy stock options which are typically linked to the S&P 500, or may be linked to other indices as well. The insurance company watches the activity of the stock options and if at the end of the cycle the stock goes up, they buy, **and credit you and themselves with a share of the gain**. If it goes down, they walk away and absorb any losses, not charging you the client for those losses; one of the incentives for the insurance company to do business this way is by contractually setting a CAP with you on the percentage of gain which you the client can receive.

EXAMPLE: If the percentage of gain in a cycle was to be, say, 10%, but the established contractual CAP set by the insurance company with you the customer is 7%, you receive the benefit of the 7%. Through its own investments, plus the use of adjustable CAP Rates and Participation Rates, et cetera, the insurance company makes its profits, for taking all the risks on your behalf.

Gambler/Investor
vs.
Conservative Saver?

Which are you??

The mathematics of "losing" vs. "not losing."

To further illustrate the impact of LOSING vs. NOT LOSING let's assume you have

$100,000 and the market goes down 25%, how much do you need to get back to $100,000? Most people say, 25% - right? Wrong! It is 33% because 33% of 75,000 (the amount you are left with after a 25% loss), is $100,000 (just about). What if the market goes down 50%? What do you need to get back to $100,000? Right! 100%! You need to double your money to break even!

Have we seen the market go down by 40 or 50% in one shot?

Of course, many times.

Have we ever seen it go up by 100% in one shot?

Right. Never.

Isn't it interesting though, how when the market losses and gains are presented by Wall Street (and the media), they will typically say something like "on Wednesday the market took a dive, but by Friday it recovered back to its same level". Good for it, but not for you! As we have just seen, mathematically, even though it went back to the same level, your money was left behind. ☹

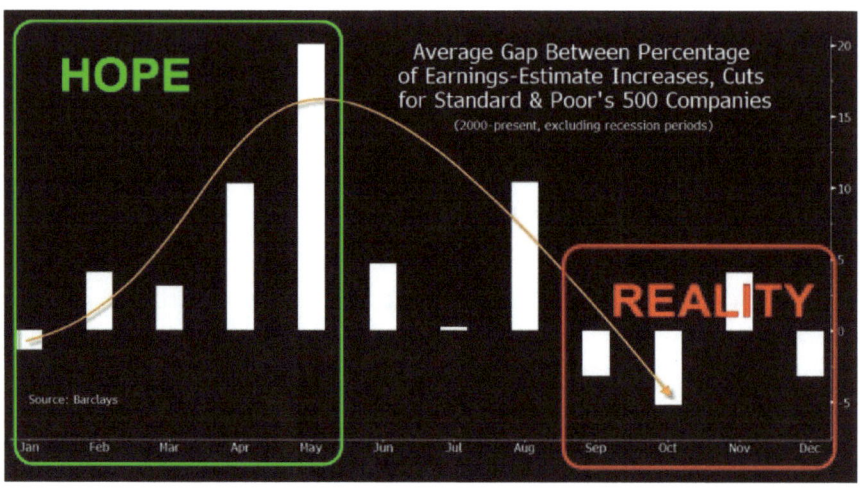

% Lost	% Needed to Break Even
10	11
20	24
30	47
40	76
50	100

Now I will show you what never losing means **VERSUS** a variable **(RISKY)** market.

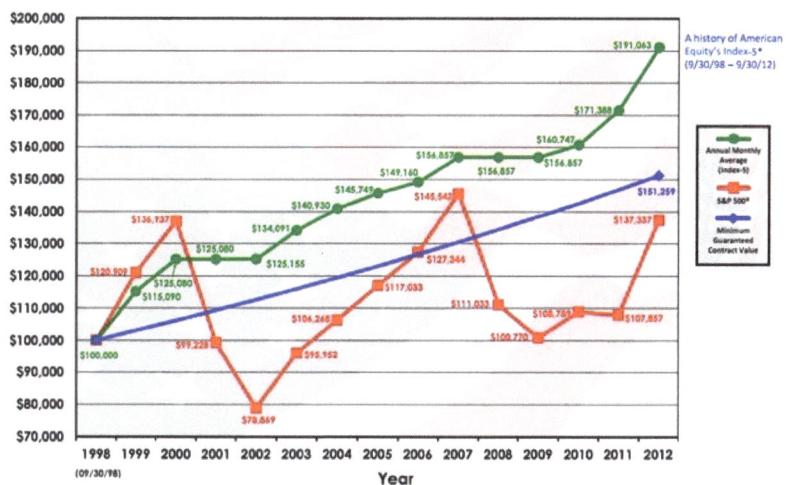

Also, there is a **HUGE** difference between 'Average Returns' and 'Actual Returns'. The stock market, Wall Street, and the News ALL quote average returns, which mislead you into believing better things are happening with your money, than actually are…

You see, rate of return is actually comprised of two types of return: average return and actual return. The difference is simple: **losses**. When calculating an average return, gains and losses are equal in weight. In other words, a +50% followed by a -50% leaves an average return of zero. This part is pretty straightforward. $100k invested would still equal $100k if you average zero. The interesting thing is, when you **calculate the actual return**. Let's take the same example and actually play around with some easy math; we'll see what really happens. When you take $100k and add 50%, your account will be worth $150k. Now if you take the $150k and subtract 50%, then you only have $75k. That is a 25% loss from your original $100k. Why is this? It's because the **losses are subtracted as a percentage of the higher amount**, where your money was before the dive, and the gains are on the smaller amount that your money became after the crash. **Any time you have one year of losses your average**

return will not equal your actual return. It will be less. And losses have greater weight and impact on your actual dollars than gains do.

Example

Example - Beginning Balance $10,000

	Beginning Balance	% Change	Ending Balance
Year 1	$10,000	+40%	$14,000
Year 2	$14,000	-40%	$8,400
Year 3	$8,400	+20%	$10,080
Year 4	$10,080	-30%	$7,056
Year 5	$7,050	+30%	$9,173
	Average Return = +20%	versus	-8.3% Actual Return

Any time you have a year of losses during any time period, your **average return will not equal your actual return**

Here's another way to see it in practice. Let's review the Dow Jones from 1930 to 2012. If you add up every number and divide it by 81 years, the return 'averages' 6.31%; however, if you do the math like we did above, you get an 'actual' return of 4.31%. Why is this so important? If you invested $1,000 back in 1930 at 6.31% you would have $142k. But when you calculate the **actual** return of 4.31%... you would only have $30k!

As you can see from this example, the impact of looking at the average returns as the only measurement could be **devastating**. This, however, is only one part of the equation. It also depends on **when** the losses happen, and **when** you need to start taking out money… But that's for another day…

Meanwhile, think about this for a moment... Does this make sense to you? For basic needs, one should have at least (3) guaranteed sources of income. If you still like to play (risk) your money, isn't it wise to only risk your vacations, and not your food or housing? See the four square chart below:

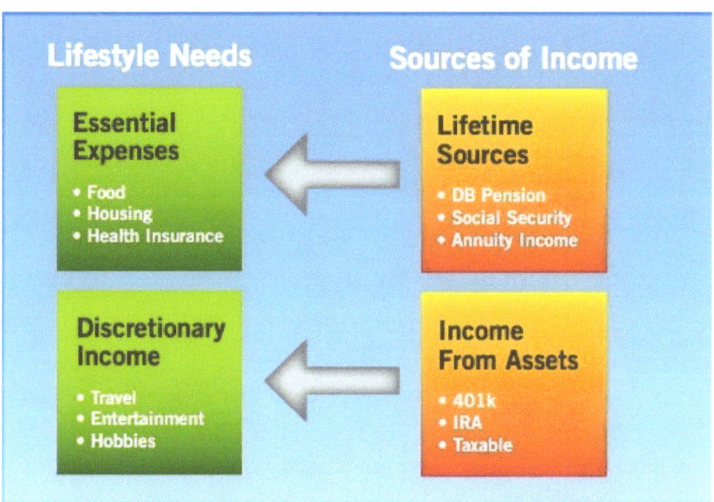

Some additional thoughts about the cost of health care:

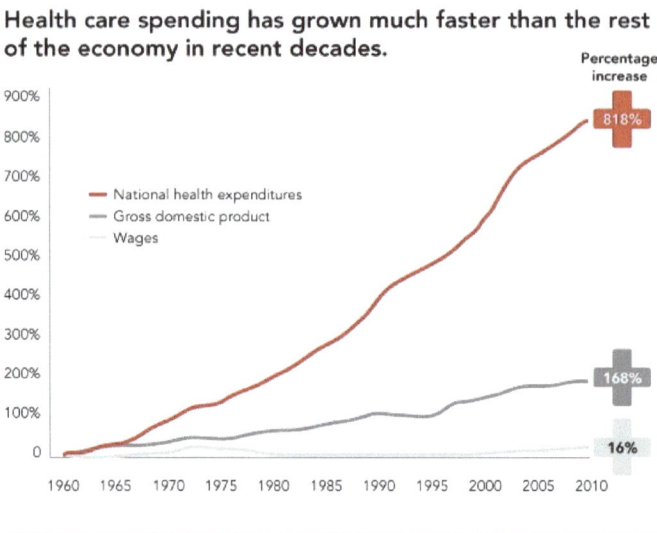

Health care spending has grown much faster than the rest of the economy in recent decades.

Percentage increase

900%

800%

700%

600%

500%

400%

300%

200%

100%

0

— National health expenditures
— Gross domestic product
— Wages

818%

168%

16%

1960 1965 1970 1975 1980 1985 1990 1995 2000 2005 2010

Sources: McKinsey, "Accounting for the Cost of U.S. Health Care" (2011), Center for American Progress

THE HUFFINGTON POST

Disclaimer

This is for informational/educational purposes only and is not to be considered specific financial advice in any way related to any individual person.

Two Separate And Unique Cash Accumulation Vehicles Offered By Life Insurance Companies

II. Maximum Tax Advantaged Life Insurance –
Tax-Free Income For Life --

Taxes -- How To Avoid Them, Not Evade Them!! ;)

"I don't want life insurance!" Yes, you do! And **it's some new information that you may not have been aware of, which will clearly show you why you do, you do, you really, really do!** ☺

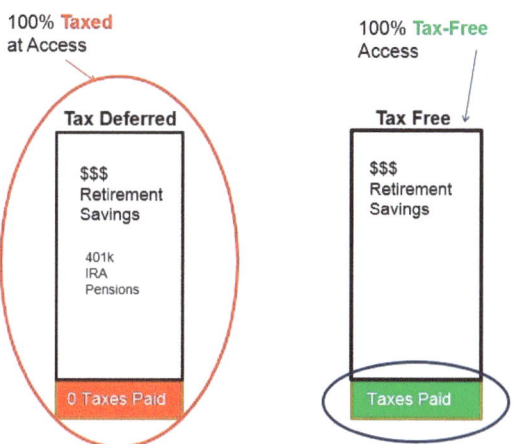

Maximum Tax Advantaged Life Insurance is **not** the life insurance you know. it's not the life insurance that you usually hear about in the news, on the Ms. "Term Only Show" (fact: most of her money is in zero-coupon Grade A, tax-free municipal bonds – **not** the stock market or a 401(K), (fact: she used to sell Single Premium Whole Life Insurance), on 'Angry' Money (hehe), or on the street corner…

What we are describing is an **IRS** and **Congress approved** complex financial tool that can be used, and is used, as a tax-shelter for cash accumulation and tax-free income on distribution. Say again?

Okay, I'll explain, but first some more interesting facts regarding Ms. Term Only's advice. We're not saying anything good or bad here, we are just stating facts. You may come to your own conclusions.

The fact is, Ms. Term Only's' own employers', and its executives, actually purchased Tax Advantaged Life Insurance Policies for themselves. Here is a brief list of just some of the executives and their annual premiums which are placed into Cash Value Permanent Life Insurance:
This information was obtained via their proxy statement filed with the FCC a couple of years back. It printed that: Company 'X's CEO pays $122,000 per year for cash whole life insurance.

The CFO pays a premium of $62,000 per year.

A Vice Chairman of Company 'X' pays premiums of $105 thousand per year.

Another vice chairman of 'X' pays $79,000 per year and the head of 'X1' contributes $506,000 per year into cash value whole life insurance.

(You can find similar examples, and many, many more astonishing facts in the book "The Pirates of Manhattan", by Barry James Dyke)

Here's my last word on this, I promise. It's just that it is so important to know all of what is happening. So, Ms. Term Only, actually used to sell a similar type of Cash Value Life Insurance called Single Premium Whole Life policies (these were structured a bit differently, yet many of the same benefits remained). She did seminars on it, and even spoke on the radio in favor of it. Here is a quote from Ms. Term Only, in an article for Success.com in 2009:

"I started to specialize in an investment called single premium whole life," 'Ms. T' said. "I loved it!" She described the product as a legal tax loophole that allowed people to invest with little to no risk and respectable returns. "It was one of the greatest investments around."

Ms. 'T' opened her own firm in 1987 and used her knowledge of single premium whole life policies to help her new Pacific Gas &Electric retirees. "It was the most brilliant thing I've ever done, and I made a fortune. And the people made a fortune…" she said.

Okay, so that's that. We're not saying anything good or bad, we are just stating facts. And although some people out in TV land say that they "hate" people and "hate" things that they publically don't agree with, we never say we "hate" anyone or anything. Hate is a very strong negative word and feeling, and is best avoided at all costs. Just our opinion.

Now, back to the matter at hand… as you can see, when structured properly, and according to five **Main IRS Rules Regarding Life**

Insurance, an *Indexed Universal Life Insurance Contract* performs much like a Mutual Fund only **without** the ***capital gains tax*** or ***the income tax*** (upon distribution), *and without the hidden management fees*, and without the ***market risk to principal and interest***. You'll never take two steps forward only to fall five steps back!

As America's CPA, Ed Slott says "Life Insurance is an Investment and is the single best use of the IRS Tax code to AVOID taxes."

gregory@BeverlyHillsPrivatePensions.com

The five MAIN IRS Rules are:

TEFRA 1982, DEFRA 1984, TAMRA 1988, Guideline Single Premium (GSP), and MEC (Modified Endowment Contract). (For a detailed discussion of these rules and others such as: *Tax Citations: IRC Section 101, IRC Section 72(e) Rev. Rule 66-322, 1966-2 CB 123, TEFRA Section 266, DEFRA Section 221*, you may see Missed Fortune 101 by Douglas Andrew, **or just go to the IRS website and type in the aforementioned rules, citations, and codes).**

What Do These IRS Rules Mean, And How Do They Help You?

These rules achieve the following: They provide a corridor that dictates the minimum death benefit required based upon the insured's age and gender to accommodate the ultimate desired aggregate premium basis.

HUH??? In other words, when one structures these contracts in this particular way, one is *minimizing* the **death benefit (cost)** and *maximizing* the **cash accumulation (gain)**. We need the death benefit though, so that it **still** qualifies **as** life insurance so that we may reap the unique tax-favored status these contracts have.

There **are cash value life insurance contracts** called **BOLI and COLI** which stand for *Bank Owned Life Insurance, and Corporate Owned Life Insurance.*

Now, when was the last time a bank or corporation was worried about dying?

Exactly, never.

They don't "die."

So why would they want **life insurance**? Just as I said, **for the living benefits of** the unique tax-favored status it receives from the IRS. And again, when structured properly *they are used to channel money in and out on a tax-free basis.* Here is a definition directly from Investopedia:

Bank-Owned Life Insurance – BOLI

"What Does Bank-Owned Life Insurance - BOLI Mean?
A form of life insurance purchased by banks where the bank is the beneficiary, and/or owner. *This form of insurance is a tax shelter for the administering bank, as it is a tax-free funding scheme for employee benefits.*

Investopedia explains Bank-Owned Life Insurance – BOLI

Banks use BOLI contracts to fund ever-increasing employee benefits at a much cheaper rate. The process works like this: the bank sets up the contract, and then makes payments into a specialized fund set aside as the insurance trust. All employee benefits that need to be paid to particular employees covered under the plan are paid out from this fund.

All premiums paid into the fund, as well as all capital appreciation, are tax free for the bank. *Therefore, banks can use the BOLI system to fund employee benefits on a tax-free basis."*

Now, we know you are wondering… If banks can do this, why can't we? The answer is you CAN!

But these are very special contracts and most life insurance agents or financial advisors do not have the slightest idea about how to structure them. You must find a qualified professional who can **prove** that s/he is qualified to help you.

gregory@BeverlyHillsPrivatePensions.com

Index Universal Life Insurance vs. 401(k)

	IUL	401(k)
Guaranteed Minimum Returns (2-3%)	✓	✗
Guaranteed Lifetime Income	✓	✗
Tax Free Death Benefit (Lump Sum)	✓	✗
Critical Illness Protection	✓	✗
Tax Free Income After Death	✓	✗
Disability Income	✓	✗
Chronic Illness Protection	✓	✗
Downside Protection Against Stock Market Loss	✓	✗

A lot of these benefits are like getting gifts, and if you're not getting them, you're really missing out!

Chapter IV

Roth IRA Conversion

In a world preparing for higher taxes and in fear of volatile markets, one can use the *security* of a **Fixed Indexed Annuity** and **Combine It** with the *Tax-Free nature* of a **Roth IRA**.

[Do you think **future taxes** will be lower, **or higher**? If you think they will be higher, *why not* pay taxes today, so that you don't have to pay **higher taxes tomorrow**? This can also be done with an MTA Life Insurance Contract, IF you qualify].

This is what a **Roth IRA** will do for you:

It will grow your retirement savings without growing your TAX burden.

Once in the Roth IRA, you have the *opportunity* to NOT pay taxes on **any future growth or future distributions**.

The Roth IRA has **kinder / gentler rules** for YOU!

How can this be done?

The **Tax Increase Prevention And Reconciliation Act Of 2005** (the "ACT"), **makes this possible**.

Comparison of Traditional IRA or 401(k), 403(b) etc. to the Roth IRA:

In a traditional IRA or 401(k), 403(b) et cetera, you **must** :	The **Tax Increase Prevention and Reconciliation Act of 2005** (the "Act") and a **Roth IRA**:
1. Pay taxes on ALL distributions	The Act Allows highly compensated individuals with adjusted gross **incomes of $100,000 or more** to **convert** from their IRAs, 401(k)s, 403(b)s to a **Roth IRA. Previously, only those with adjusted gross incomes less than $100,000 could convert.**
2. Take Required Minimum Distributions ("RMDs") by AGE 70 ½ or face a **50% penalty!! -- use it or lose it!!!**	1. You are allowed to **pay the taxes now** (presumably at a lower rate), rather than later (when taxes are likely to increase).
Think about that for a second -- you face losing one-half of your money if you do not take a required minimum distribution on time!!	2. Withdrawals are **not** required starting at age 70½ (i.e. no RMDs!)
3. At death, beneficiaries must pay taxes on the balance they inherit.	3. At death, beneficiaries *may* **not** be taxed on the Roth IRA balance
4. As your *balance grows, so **shall** your taxes.*	As your balance grows, you have an **opportunity** *not* **to have your taxes grow on future growth or future distributions (i.e. "Tax-Free Treatment")**

Guidelines for Tax Free Treatment ("Opportunity") of your

Roth IRA:

Withdrawals are **not** taxable **IF**:

(1)   the balance is held in the Roth IRA for at least **five** years
AND:
(2)   **not** withdrawn **prior** to age 59½.

Testing your Financial Consultant:

If you're interested in finding someone who knows how to do this for you….

First, ask the financial consultant, advisor or planner if s/he is familiar with the "Tax Increase Prevention and Reconciliation Act of 2005" (the "Act").   If not, if s/he seems uncomfortable and cannot explain the Act and its provisions to you, run for the hills and find someone else!

(Don't mention the Roth Conversion until you get a positive answer and explanation of the Act with regard to the Roth Conversion).

We all have a **tremendous** opportunity to pay lower taxes now, so that we can avoid paying higher taxes later. Now is the time to do it!

www.BeverlyHillsPrivatePensions.com

CHAPTER V

The 412(e)(3) Plan For Highly Compensated Business Owners

At a time when the world is upside down, when the only thing that seems certain, is uncertainty and when business owners are struggling with taxes, asset protection and the question of an exit strategy at retirement, the 412(e)(3) is a safe haven in a tropical storm.

These are **extremely** complex plans and have many details to them in order to conform to the IRS Codes created for them.

Again, we will only briefly highlight some key points.

What Is A 412(e)(3) Fully Insured Plan?

A 412(e)(3) Fully Insured Plan, formerly known as the 412(i) Fully Insured Plan, referred to in the IRS regulations as an **"insurance contract plan,"** is a special type of *defined benefit plan*.

It is also called a "fully insured" plan…...

because due to IRS regulation, the **benefits must be guaranteed** by the insurance company. A 412(e)(3) Plan is **NOT** subject to many of the requirements that have made traditional defined benefit plans unpopular over the years. **Furthermore, these plans have become even more popular lately because changes in the tax laws over the last few years have made them more attractive**. How is that? Well, because the investments in these plans are based on fixed accounts with **retirement benefits guaranteed**, they are getting a second look now that there is so much volatility in the equity markets. Also, the IRS is allowing business owners to stuff much more of their own dollars, and much fewer dollars for their employees, into such plans.

Why Is A 412(e)(3) Plan Not Subject To The Funding Requirements Of A Traditional Defined Benefit Plan?

412(e)(3) Plans get their name from the sub-section of the tax code that provides an **exemption** to the minimum funding requirement of Section 412. As long as the plan follows certain requirements, the exemption is available.

The requirements are listed below:

- **The plan must be funded exclusively by the "purchase of individual insurance contracts."**
- The contracts must "provide for level annual premium payments."
- **The benefits provided under the plan must be "guaranteed by an insurance carrier (licensed under the laws of a State to do business with the plan) to the extent premiums have been paid."**
- The life insurance products funding the plan can have "no policy loans outstanding at any time during the plan year."

- The *exemption* to minimum funding requirements *is granted because* an **insurance company is guaranteeing the benefits "to the extent premiums have been paid."**

How Does The Insurance Company Guarantee The Benefits?

412(e)(3) Plans are funded with specific insurance products (annuities and/or life insurance.) These are *fixed products* which have a guaranteed and a current interest rate. After the retirement benefit is decided upon, the initial contributions to the plan are calculated using the guaranteed interest rates in the insurance products. Any life insurance dividends or excess annuity interest *are required to be used* to **reduce** the following year's contributions!

There are *many* more AMAZING benefits to these plans including being safe from predators —er–ah, I mean creditors. Hehe. ;)

Again, we are just *briefly educating you on cash accumulation vehicles* that exist and that are **guaranteed** so that you can be aware of something that you may not have previously been aware of.

We hope this has been helpful to you.

If these things interest you, it is now up to you to find a qualified, knowledgeable and experienced professional to help you to achieve your goals. **If** you already have your own **very** well educated insurance professional who is well trained in this area of defined benefit plans, by all means, **use her/him.**

If not, feel free to **reach out to us**, regardless of what state you live in. We will do our best to help you get any questions answered and get you set up.

Thank you for your interest and thank you for listening. ☺

CHAPTER VI

Some Additional Useful Information

Bonds–Defined, And Comments

Bond

What Does the Term "Bond" Mean?

A "Bond" is a *debt investment* in which an **investor loans** *money* to an entity (corporate or governmental) that borrows the funds for a defined period of time at a fixed interest rate. Bonds are used by companies, municipalities, states and U.S. and foreign governments to finance a variety of projects and activities.

Bonds are commonly referred to as *"fixed-income securities"* and are **one** of **The Three Main Asset Classes**, along with **"stocks"** and **"cash equivalents"**.

Investopedia explains *Bond*

The indebted entity (issuer - "Borrower") issues a bond that states the interest rate (coupon) that will be paid and when the loaned funds (bond principal) are to be returned (maturity date). Interest on bonds is usually paid every six months (semi-annually).

The main categories of bonds are Corporate Bonds, Municipal Bonds, and U.S. Treasury Bonds, Notes and Bills (which are collectively referred to as simply **"Treasuries").**

Two features of a bond **- credit quality and duration -** are the *principal determinants* of a bond's interest rate. Bond maturities range from a 90-day Treasury bill to a 30-year government bond. Corporate and Municipals are typically in the 3 to 10-year range.

Security and/or Safety of Bonds

As for the security and or safety of bonds, although they are **not** in themselves *guaranteed cash accumulation vehicles* most investors find bonds, especially high grade corporate or government bonds to be **extremely** safe and secure. Empirically, we would say look at **what the BEST risk managers in the world** invest in and you may have your answer. For example, insurance companies as a whole, have as their main investments, high grade corporate and or government bonds. The life insurance industry is a 400 year old industry with a less than one percent failure rate. No other industry can even come close to those statistics! Thus, you may draw your own conclusions.

CHAPTER VII

10 Secrets about CDs You'll Never Hear From A Bank

Given today's new tax laws, people living longer in retirement, the cost of probate, inflation, the volatility of the stock market and the availability of many new and innovative products, it makes it very difficult for most people to keep up-to-date and sort through it all.

This chapter is intended to provide our friends, family and clients with an overview of the information they need to help them understand some of the many complex financial issues we all face in today's economic environment.

Today, many people are turning to a brand new line of tax-deferred annuities, as a foundation of their overall financial plan, in place of stocks or mutual funds, certificates of deposit or municipal bonds. Think of it as trading in one of the first cell phones, from over 30 years ago, for a new smart phone that does everything but drive your car, clean the house, and take care of the kids! If cell phones have come this far in the same time period... isn't it time to upgrade your 401(k)s, 403(b)s, 457s, IRAs et cetera... ???

Why would you want to get left behind, when you can easily get with the times!

Why? That is what this chapter is all about. It also ties together much of what we explained in earlier chapters.

Common Concerns of Retirees

While there are a number of different ways retirees approach their income needs in retirement, we have found that they have the following common concerns:

- **Preservation of Principal** - They don't know how long they're going to be retired, and they don't want to outlive their money.
- **Safety of Investments** - They want to make sure their income is there each and every month. So, they can't afford to risk losing any of their investment principal.
- **Minimization of Income Taxes** - No one likes to pay needless income taxes, especially retirees.
- **Growth of Income** - As the cost of living increases; they want their incomes to increase.

#1: CD Interest Rates Are Too Low

Currently, CD rates are averaging 1.80% for a FIVE YEAR CD, or lower for shorter periods. And if you are in a 30% tax bracket, your net after tax return is only 1.26%. It'll take over 57 years for your money to double!

Ouch!

In the past few years, the inflation rate has averaged around 4.0% down to 1.6%, allegedly, but have you checked the cost of gas, eggs, and milk lately? After adjusting your CD investment return for taxes and inflation, **you are losing money**. CDs are only one step up from savings accounts and money market funds, which offer the lowest investment returns. **If you want to have more income and more buying power in the future, then you can't afford to have your money in a CD.**

See Example Below for Real Rate Of Return...

Year CD Rate Less Taxes Inflation Net Return

2014   1.80   -   30%   -   1.6%   =   (1.24)

#2: You Can Get Higher Returns Than CDs And Still Guarantee Your Initial Investment

Did you know that fixed deferred annuities have averaged, in the worst case scenario around 3.0% annually, and up to 6.5% annually in some cases, over the past thirteen years? That's twice the average rate of inflation. Fixed Deferred Annuities, as evidenced by their performance history, consistently outperform other alternatives - such as CDs, savings accounts and money market funds. In fact, in comparison to these rates, the ACTUAL return from the stock market was out performed by these Fixed Deferred Annuities. And Fixed Deferred Annuities have been issued in the United States since 1812. Today, they represent one of the most popular cash accumulation vehicles used for retirement and other long term needs by investors seeking conservative growth of their assets. There are over 49 million individual and supplementary annuity contracts in existence, and rising! While annuities have been bought by the public and corporations in the U.S. for over 190 years, their popularity has grown dramatically, primarily during the past decade.

#3: CD Surrender Penalties Go On Forever, And Start Over With Each Renewal

CDs charge a surrender penalty on any money you withdraw prior to maturity. Each time you renew your CD, you start a new surrender penalty period. **So, with a CD, the penalties really go on forever**. Like CDs, fixed deferred annuities have a penalty for early surrender. However, unlike CDs, their penalties reduce each year and generally end in 5 to 10 years. Most deferred annuities allow you penalty-free withdrawals of 10% or more each year. You can usually withdraw 100% of the money penalty free if you are terminally ill or you need it for nursing home care. Of course, there can be a 10% tax penalty for withdrawals from your annuity prior to age 59 1/2.

#4: Safety CDs vs. Annuities

Do insurance companies have FDIC? No.
Are they just as safe? Yes.
A little historical perspective may be helpful.

Insurance is highly regulated by each state. This high level of regulation for safety's sake was largely a result of the Armstrong Investigations in 1905, which really did not have nice things to say about the insurance industry way back then, at the time. So, heavy solvency-oriented state regulation was the result. **Insurance companies must, by law, cover at least 100% of their liabilities with reserves, hence, the term "100% legal reserve life insurance company."** There are also regulations as to the percentage that can be held in certain forms of assets. This system has produced a remarkable overall record of solvency and safety.

The FDIC
The Federal Deposit Insurance Corporation is pledged to pay depositors, upon the default of a bank, up to $250,000. FDIC is normally funded by the banks themselves. (It is an assessment to member banks.) But more recently, taxpayers have been asked to pay also, because bank defaults have been higher recently. Savings & Loan defaults covered by FSLIC have been greater, as has the bill (hundreds of billions) to the taxpayers. All of this history is merely to point out that banking, by its very nature, has some risk. (a 10 to 1 risk, actually)

Will FDIC or FSLIC always pay in full? Yes.
Does FDIC or FSLIC always pay right away? No.

All 50 states have something similar to FDIC for insurance policies and annuities. They are called "state guarantee funds." Only the District of Columbia is, at this time, without a life-health guarantee association.

#5: CDs Can Be Seized By Creditors

If you are sued for any reason, your CD can be seized by a creditor. *Example: if you are involved in a car accident or you have to file for bankruptcy.* In most states, fixed deferred annuities are protected from all creditors, even in bankruptcy. **That's real safety**.

#6: With A CD, You Pay Income Taxes On The Interest Every Year

With a CD, every year you receive a 1099, and pay taxes, whether you withdraw your interest or not.

Tax Advantages Of Annuities

With a deferred annuity, you pay NO taxes while your money is compounding. You can pay a lower tax on random withdrawals because you control the tax year in which the withdrawals are made, and you only pay taxes on the interest withdrawn. Tax deferral gives you control over your taxes. The longer you can postpone your taxes, the greater your gain when compared to what you would make with a fully taxable account.

Why Pay Taxes On Interest Income When You Don't Have To?

Especially when you can earn Triple Compounding interest!

1. Earn Interest on Your **Principal.**
2. Earn Interest on Your **Interest.**
3. Earn Interest on the **Federal and State Tax Dollars** that you would have paid.

Tax Deferral
Your legal right to choose when, if ever, during your lifetime you pay "income taxes" on your interest income.

#7: CD Interest Can Make Up To 85% Of Your Social Security Income Taxable

You are required to report your CD interest income on your 1040. Your CD income is then combined with all your other income to determine your "modified adjusted gross income". If your "modified adjusted gross income" exceeds $34,000 (single) or $44,000 (married), then 85% of your Social Security check is taxable. Income between $25,000 and $34,000 (single) or between $32,000 and $44,000 (married) will cause up to 50% of your Social Security check to be taxed.

Annuity deferred interest is not reportable on your 1040.

Accordingly, the interest is not used to determine your "modified adjusted gross income". Annuities provide a special tax advantage for retirees. Many retirees are paying income taxes on 50% to 85% of their Social Security check when they could avoid it. If you want to see if you're paying taxes on your Social Security, look at line 20b of your Tax Return (1040a).

#8: CDs Are Subject To Probate

Probate is the legal process of validating a Will, paying debts, and distributing assets after death. Generally, after you die, most of your assets, including CDs, will go through probate. This includes all the assets you own in your name and those paid to your estate. Obviously, assets in a **Trust** do not go through probate. It's just that many millions of people, never 'get around' to setting up a trust to save their beneficiaries years of headaches, hardship and loss of money and assets.

Deferred Annuities Avoid Probate

After you die, the accumulated funds within your annuity will be transferred to your named beneficiaries, avoiding the expense, delay, frustration and publicity of the probate process.

Annuities Offer More Advantages and Annuities Are Incontestable.

Heirs, family members and creditors can and do contest Wills, Trusts and the distribution of other assets going through probate, slowing up the process and adding additional expenses.

Annuities Are Private.

Unlike Trusts, Wills and the probate process, which are a matter of public record, you can leave assets to a friend, a favorite relative or a charity without upsetting the remaining heirs.

Annuities Provide Immediate Cash Resources.

Your family has the money they need to live on while they are waiting for distribution of other assets.

Annuities Provide Control From The Grave.

You can specify whether your heirs receive a lump sum payment or a guaranteed monthly income.

#9: Annuities Can Provide A Guaranteed Income For The Rest Of Your Life

Many years ago, many employees had a company pension. Today most of them don't. That's why a growing number of retirees are taking a second look at **fixed immediate annuities** as a way of creating a predictable, guaranteed income. 'It's a do-it-yourself pension, for a do-it-yourself world,' Recent findings from the TIAA-CREF Institute, the research arm of the world's largest retirement system for teachers, found that a retirement portfolio divided between an immediate annuity and a managed portfolio could supercharge retirement security, providing both more certain, and larger payouts than from a fully managed portfolio. (Kiplinger's Personal Finance 10/01)

Fixed Immediate annuities provide many great advantages:

- **Security** - the annuity provides stable, lifetime income which can never be outlived or which may be guaranteed for a specified period.
- **Simplicity** - the annuitant does not have to manage his investments, watch markets, report interest or dividends.
- **Higher Returns** - the interest rates used by insurance companies to calculate immediate annuity income are generally higher than CD or Treasury rates, and since part of the principal is returned with each payment, greater amounts are received than would be provided by interest alone.
- **Preferred Tax Treatment** - it lets you postpone paying taxes on some of the earnings you've accrued in a fixed "tax deferred" annuity when rolled into a fixed immediate annuity (only the portion attributable to interest is taxable income, the bulk of the payments are non-taxable return of principal). Obviously, the best situation is to use a ROTH FIA, or an MTA, so that no-taxes need to be paid in the future, but if your situation is such that that is not possible, then this is a viable and prudent option.
- **Safety of Principal** - funds are guaranteed by assets of insurer and not subject to the fluctuations of financial markets. And there are...
  No Sales or Administrative Charges (on the basic account, with no riders).

#10: Today You Can Get Stock Market Type Returns, Without Risking Your Principal!

A new innovation for the new millennium...

Fixed Indexed Annuity

Can you imagine an investment that provides the long-term potential growth of the stock market, without the downside risk?
Plus, your principal and a minimum interest rate are guaranteed.

Guarantee Provision

- Once you make a premium payment, you will never have less in your account than your premium payment.
- Once interest has been credited to your fixed indexed annuity, the value of your annuity will never decrease, even if the stock market goes down.

Interest Rate

The interest credited to your fixed indexed annuity is tied to the performance of the S&P 500 Index. Actual 10-Year Compound Annual Returns for the S&P 500 Index, Standard & Poor's 500 stock index is calculated by Standard & Poor's Corp. Does not include dividends. Based on actual dates 12/31/95-12/31/05.

Remember, the S&P 500 Index has consistently out-performed the vast majority of mutual funds.

"Standard & Poor's", "S&P 500", "Standard & Poor's 500" and "500" are trademarks of The McGraw-Hill Companies, Inc. and have been licensed for use by companies offering Equity Index Annuities. The product is not sponsored, endorsed, sold or promoted by Standard & Poor's (a number placed in parenthesis, IS 'Accounting Math' for a "negative value)

2000	2001	2002	2003	2004	2005	2006	2007	2008	2009
14.85	10.66	7.28	9.08	10.19	7.29	6.71	4.36	(3.03)	(2.72)

The Tortoise vs. The Hare

Equity investments such as stocks or mutual funds frequently have flashes of brilliance, but occasionally fall back. Most investors would be pleased with gains in four out of every five years. But, do the great years offset those years with a poor or a negative return? This is a question frequently asked by persons purchasing fixed deferred annuities, and trying to contrast the level performance with stocks, mutual funds, or variable annuities. If you started with a $100,000 deposit, which strategy would produce a higher cash balance in five years? The answer is that both of these strategies would produce exactly the same result of $147,000. What does this tell us?

Consistency out-produces flashes of brilliance!
This poses an important question;

"Where is the justification for taking the much higher risk associated with equity investments?"

So, are Low Interest Rates, Volatile Stock Market Fluctuations, Income Taxes and Inflation Reducing Your Standard Of Living?

Depending on your situation, there are some simple, proven, time-tested strategies you can use to increase your income now and for the future, with more guarantees and less risk.

You can beat inflation, reduce your income taxes, increase your returns and avoid the downside risks of the stock market.

We're not talking about some weird untested investment, or product that guarantees a consistent 20% or higher return. **There is no such thing**, as many retirees have unfortunately found out. What we are talking about is **Equity Management and Asset Protection**, which, quite simply, is just positioning your assets properly, in order to allow yourself to get more from what you have.

It's just simple math!

But, I Already Have An Advisor.
Many of the people we help do/did have a stock broker, an accountant, an old insurance agent or friend who has guided them in their financial matters. Unfortunately, while in most cases these advisors were well intentioned, they generally had a narrow perspective of the problems and solutions. The advice they gave was based mainly on their limited area of expertise and/or what has worked for them personally in the past. Unfortunately, what worked for them in the past, in many cases, was not the best solution for the people they were trying to help, now, in the present.

The world has changed, and so have financial markets, strategies, and insurance. So, yes, these people who advised you, had some success. But, their situation could have been much better... We take a Personalized, Holistic Approach to Finances. You're not a 'cookie', so you shouldn't have a one-size-fits all 'cookie cutter' plan, should you? You deserve Personalized Attention!

What Does It Cost?

All our initial consultations are free. There is never a cost or obligation to you.

Our Guarantee
It's very simple. We do all the work. We'll review your situation and make our recommendations to you. Then it's up to you to make the decision to do business with us. The only cost to you is a little bit of your time.

So, What's the Next Step?
Let us ask you, is it worth 15 to 20 initial minutes, of your time to see if you can have **more money to spend, now and in the future?** Would you like to see if you can **significantly reduce or eliminate your income taxes?** Would you like to **stop worrying about running out of money?** Would you like to **have more money to do more of the things you have always wanted to do?** Would you like to have more trips to see your grandchildren, a new car, more golf or whatever else you've wanted to do? Remember, there is no risk, no cost and no obligation, just education. You have nothing to lose and everything to gain!

Call us today!

Seriously, do it. It will be the single best and most important decision you make this year!

Call Now Toll Free 877-855-1881

Whether we direct you *elsewhere*, or to us, the thing that matters is that you get the safe, qualified help that you need. Not quite sure...?

Some More Painful Facts:

- The Wall Street illusionists have been pulling the wool over everyone's eyes for decades! You take all the risk, and they get the rewards, whether you make money or not!

- "What's worse, the typical 401(k) **will steal an average of nearly $155,000 from each worker** over a lifetime of saving." Hidden 401(k) Fees: The Great Retirement Plan Rip-Off By Adam J. Wiederman, The Motley Fool

- A recent study revealed that, **for the past 190 years**, *American stocks have averaged a REAL annual return of only 1.4 percent!* The study did not deduct, commissions or taxes. "Stock market's real return? Paltry," by Anthony Mirhaydari, MSN Money, February 1, 2010.

- *The typical equity mutual fund investor has actually been losing one percent a year for the past 20 years, after adjusting for inflation.* DALBAR's 2008 Quantitative Analysis of Investor Behavior.

- Beating The S&P 500
"Over the 15 years ending October 31, 2005, 94.28% *of actively managed funds did worse than the S&P 500*" John Stossel, author and reporter ABC's 20/20. Myths Lies and Downright Stupidity by John Stossel.

- Beating The Market
"While 94% of funds failed to beat the S&P 500 the tiny 6% of funds that did beat the market do not do it consistently. In other words, picking a fund that beat the market last year does not mean it will beat the market in the coming years."

"...beating the market average (S&P 500) has proven to be impossible to accomplish over time"- "Stop Sitting on Your Assets" by Marian Snow.

- *Fees: "Low Cost",* Growth Fund Fees in a 401(k)… Fund Mgt fees = 1.13%; Fund trading costs = 0.86%; Participant education fees = 0.75%; Administration fees = 0.15%; Custodial fees = 0.05%; Audit and legal fees = 0.05%; *Total charges = 2.99%.*
LA Times.com 3/ 27/ 07

- Time.com June 4, 2012:
"It isn't unusual to find 401(k) plans with a total cost paid by the participant exceeding 3% annually".

- Forbes.com: September 7, 2009:
"The 401(k) ReThink"
"Fee Fiascos:… *once you're in a 401(k) there's no CAP on how much the plan might skim off the top in fees...* many plans, especially those sold to small companies, can eat up roughly half of the real investment returns."

- Example of those Cancerous Fees
If you contribute $1,000 a month for 30 years and earn a 7% return, you will accumulate $1,219,979. Run this at 5.5% -- *less only 1.5% fees* -- and you will have $913,617. • *That's $306,362 or 25% of YOUR total gain went to Wall Street!*

- Replace Higher Expense Fees, with Lower Ones:

In the above example, the *50 year total sent to Wall Street would have been $580,447.* This money is totally lost, because you would never earn, gain, or receive income on it. *By contrast life insurance expenses for those 50 years would have been only $75,000, and with zero tax!*

- **The insurance company doesn't punish you for increasing your account balance and succeeding!**

"The industry has lost its way. We have turned a very good profession into a business which is good for the business but not for the investor." by John Bogle, New York Times, November 2, 2003; Founder and former CEO Vanguard.

"The truth of the matter is that over time, the vast majority - approximately 80 percent - of the mutual funds under-perform the overall stock market." The Motley Fool.
What does all that mean for you, your money and your future.

gregory@BeverlyHillsPrivatePensions.com

If you want a FREE review of your situation, and you cannot find a knowledgeable and experienced advisor near you.... call us. Just pick up the phone and dial:

TOLL FREE: 877-855-1881

And just ask for:

Gregory Pavlidis

Meet The Experts– Autobiographies

Who are we, and why do we do what we do? Hi, I am Gregory Pavlidis & I own and founder of Beverly Hills Private Pensions. This, among other things, is an educational platform that serves our communities by educating and providing much needed financial literacy, and increasing financial awareness, by sharing *Un-conventional Money Secrets* that have been tested, and proven safe. Sometimes we work together on projects that we feel will greatly benefit the general public, like the aforementioned. Now a bit about me.

<u>Gregory Pavlidis: B.A., M.S.</u>

I lived in Long Island, New York until August of 1999 when, after completing my Master's Degree in Mathematics and Education from Long Island University, I relocated to Southern California. I also received my Bachelor's Degree in Economics from the same University. In addition to my degrees, I also have my Life Insurance License and had obtained my Series 6, 63 and 65 Licenses. I let them expire because I never had any intention of using them. I just wanted to show, I could pass the tests, AND I would tell clients "I'm licensed to lose your money, but I'd rather not", so let's work on the fixed side of the fence. And of course, then I would help with protecting their money, with guaranteed, fixed strategies... as opposed to the SEC side, which specializes in losing their clients' money. This is something that has been done by many advisers under the SECs dark shadow. They've done it by risking and losing their clients' money in the stock market, daily, monthly annually, and over decades!

Also, in addition to our other aforementioned qualifications, I am nationally recognized as Certified Financial Education Instructors through the National Financial Educators Council (NFEC).

Anyway, while teaching High School Mathematics, I noticed that even the well-educated, upper middle-class parents of my students were grappling with day-to-day financial survival. So, I decided the best way to utilize my skills in education, economics and mathematics was to aid the public through the financial services industry. I realized I could better serve my community by helping parents to build financial security, thereby stabilizing their homes and families. I strongly believe in the power of accurate and factual information, and I do not just manage my clients' accounts, I teach them **how and why** their money is best placed in one vehicle or another. I educate and empower people with accurate information for Retirement Safety.

In my little spare time, I like to spend time with friends and family, go for trips up Pacific Coast Highway, hike, bicycle ride, and travel to other countries. Fiji is my next destination!

One of my best friends got married there, and the photos he showed, and stories he told were unreal!

I love nature, animals, and doing what I can to keep my 'footprint' on the environment to a minimum. I really love to get out there and live! There is SO much to see. Yet, I also enjoy a quiet night home, with a book.

Now that you know a little about us personally, let's get to the business at hand...

We specialize in helping people optimize assets, enhance net worth, set up instant estates and minimize or eliminate taxes on distribution when retirement comes. And in a retirement world gone wrong, one that has eliminated the predictability and security of our senior years, by eliminating most company pensions, we help to convert risky, lazy, underperforming, unpredictable market based 401(k)s, 403(b)s, IRAs, Mutual Funds, Stocks, Bonds, et cetera, into safe, secure, guaranteed, predictable Private Pensions, with taxes paid either now, or in the future, and with incomes you can never outlive! We also help you do things right from the start, if you haven't put your money at risk, we help create the New Private Pensions for you from the get-go, because we know that the best ideas, the best plans and the best things in life are the simple ones. Simple & Safe. ☺

www.BeverlyHillsPrivatePensions.com

'Providing New Solutions in Financial Literacy'

Lastly, please allow us to add, that we've been in the Financial Services and Insurance industries for close to two decades and counting.

There is one more thing we would like to mention, that we're really happy about, because it helps so many people achieve stability, security, and tranquility.

If you would allow us to share with you, a few details about our philosophy…

After I worked for quite some time in the industry, and after realizing the massive financial literacy need that people in society have, and after realizing that we have the same goals and hopes when it comes to helping to spread the **simple truths** of **Un-conventional Money Secrets** we decided to create a medium, whereby we could reach as many people as possible, and properly educate them, so that they would be well equipped to help themselves.

As Owner and Co-Founder of *Beverly Hills Private Pensions*, I specialize in helping people to maximize the growth of their money and to receive Lifetime Retirement Income, while minimizing risk and income taxes. Although we work with many different groups, like Law Enforcement, Fire Departments, Schools, Small Business Owners, large multi-national corporations, the entertainment industry and many other demographics, it is through working with retirees that we have discovered that people are not enjoying their retirement years as much as they could or should. Why? Because they are holding back due to the fear of outliving their money. It's a very real and valid fear for everyone. We see it every day.

We understand it. And we believe we can help put your mind at ease with some simple, time tested, proven and GUARANTEED money management strategies. *"We help guarantee your retirement, we help guarantee your future."*[TM]

Whether you are already retired, or you are planning to retire soon, **or** retirement is a long way off... *wouldn't it make sense to position at least some of your money* in a way as to **minimize your income taxes** and **maximize your income potential for the future?** Wouldn't it make sense to replace your fear of the unknown, with at **one guarantee?**

Please, give us a call if you would like more information about **how you can have the retirement you have always seen and felt in your dreams.** Remember, there's no cost, no obligation, just education.

Sincerely,

Gregory Pavlidis
Beverly Hills Private Pensions

Also, some of the wonderful MTAs (or as the Time Magazine Article calls it, "Life Insurance Pension Plan", have things called "Accelerated Benefit Riders". Some companies charge for them, some don't. Either way, they are amazing because with the Terminal Rider alone, you could access up to 90% of the face value tax-free to use as you wish/need. There are also, Critical and Chronic Illness Riders that are included in the better plans. Make sure to find out the details on these gems!

'Where Your Retirement Dreams Become Reality'

Here are just a few of the ways you'll benefit, by strategically repositioning your investments;

- Pay **No Taxes** on the growth of your money until you actually use it.
- Set up a **Tax-Advantaged Plan** that can provide significant additional wealth for you in retirement - **all tax free!**
- Grow your retirement savings by sharing in the up-side of the stock market, without down-side risk, and both your principal and interest are 100% guaranteed!
- Protect your assets from law-suits, predators (creditors), opportunists and **probate!**
- Avoid being taxed on your hard-earned Social Security benefits.

7 out of 10 seniors are **unnecessarily** paying taxes on their Social Security Benefits! Stop the Madness!

Call Now Toll Free 877-855-1881

Contact:

Gregory Pavlidis

Beverly Hills Private Pensions

"Providing New Solutions in Financial Literacy"

Address:

9701 Wilshire Blvd.

Suite 1000

Beverly Hills, CA 90212

Phone: 877-855-1881

Email:

gregory@BeverlyHillsPrivatePensions.com

Website: www.BeverlyHillsPrivatePensions.com

Disclaimer

This is for informational/educational purposes only and is not to be considered specific financial advice in any way related to any individual person.